Forces

Contents

Revision

Task 1

Make a force spotter badge

 Design and make your own force spotter badge.

▶ **Think about**

How do I know a force is working on something?

What will I use to make my badge?

PCM 1

Write down your ideas like this:
I know a force is working on something because ...

Task 2 — Be a force spotter

▶ Remember

You know a force is working when you see something:

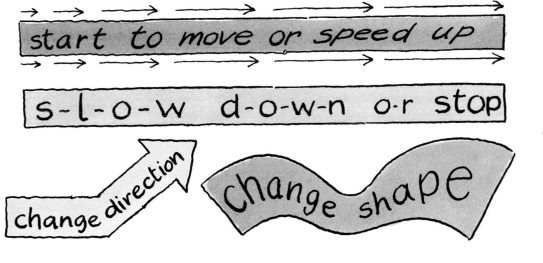

start to move or speed up

s-l-o-w d-o-w-n o-r stop

change direction

change shape

✦ Wear your force spotter badge.
Look around the classroom and school.

✦ Look for:

- two forces which make something start to move

- two forces which make something slow down or stop

- two forces which make something change direction

- two forces which make something change shape.

 PCM 2

✦ How do you know a force was working? Make a table like this or use Photocopy Master 2 to show your ideas.

Force	How I know a force was working
Make something move	
Slow down or stop	

Task 3 — *Spot the forces in action!*

- Look at the picture.
  Where are forces in action?

- Make a table.
  Record all the forces you can see.

  PCM 3

- Spot some more forces on Photocopy
  Master 3.

How do I know that a force is working?	Kind of force
ball moving	Push
dog pulling on lead	Pull

Task 4 — What can you say about forces?

- You could say ...

> Forces can change the shape of something.
> I push and pull plasticine to change the shape of it.

- Now make four more speech bubbles about forces.
  Write your ideas inside each one.

Task 5 — Forces action picture!

- Paint or draw a picture to show different forces.

▶ **Think about**

> What different things can forces do?

- On your picture, show the different things that forces can do.

- Draw arrows to show the direction of each force.

► Remember

★ A force is a push or pull. A push or pull force can make something start to move. A push or pull force can change the shape of some things.

★ Magnets can push or pull some things.

★ The bigger the push or pull force, the further something moves or the more the shape of something is changed.

★ A pull force can stretch things.

★ A force can make things slow down, go faster, or stop.

Magnets can push and pull things without touching them. Magnets can repel other magnets.

Different magnets

 Collect some different magnets. What can you find out about them?

 Draw a diagram like this to show what you know. This is called a **concept map.**

different shapes

can be

MAGNETS

 Look at your concept map.

 Write down some things that you don't know about magnets.

Now write some questions about the things you would like to know about magnets.

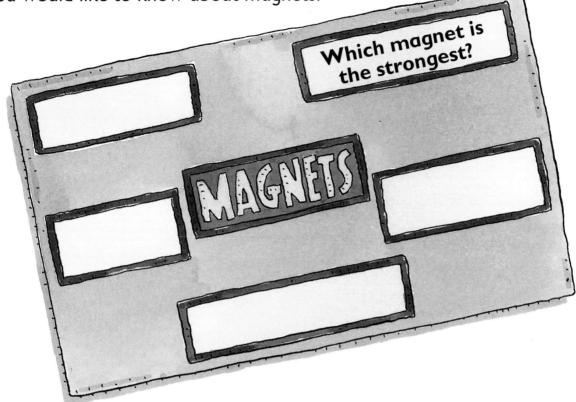

Which magnet is the strongest?

MAGNETS

Task 7 — Finding the answer

 Look at the questions you wrote for Task 6.

 How do you think you will answer your questions?

▶ Think about

Which questions can I answer by using the magnets? Which answers will I need to look up in a book?

 How will you show the answers to your questions?

 Write down your ideas. Make a table.

True or false?

▶ # Remember

Magnets sometimes have
a push force (they **repel**).

Magnets sometimes have
a pull force (they **attract**).

Magnets attract some materials.

✴ Copy the sentences on the
notepad below.
Put a 'T' by those that you think
are true.
Put an 'F' by those that you think
are false.

A magnet will pull coins.

A magnet can make a
paper-clip stand on its end.

A magnet can pull wood.

A magnet can move a
paper-clip through water
in a plastic bottle.

A magnet can move another
magnet without touching it.

✴ Now use a magnet to find out if your
predictions were correct.
(Were you right or wrong?)

Fact File

Magnets

magnetite ▶

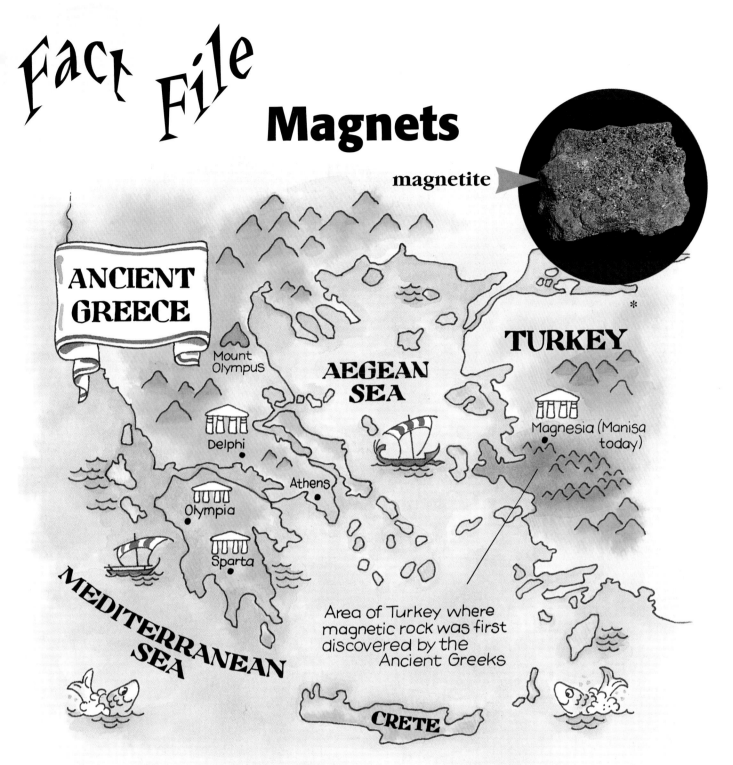

ANCIENT GREECE

Mount Olympus

Delphi

Olympia

Sparta

MEDITERRANEAN SEA

AEGEAN SEA

Athens

TURKEY

Magnesia (Manisa today)

Area of Turkey where magnetic rock was first discovered by the Ancient Greeks

CRETE

The word **magnet** comes from Magnesia in Turkey. Over 2,000 years ago, the Ancient Greeks found a special rock in Magnesia. It was special because it could make some metals stick to it.

The name given to the rock was magnetite. People used it like a magnet.

The magnets in your classroom are not made from magnetite. They are made from materials which have been made to behave like magnetite.

North pole and south pole

A magnet has two ends called poles.
There is a north pole and a south pole.

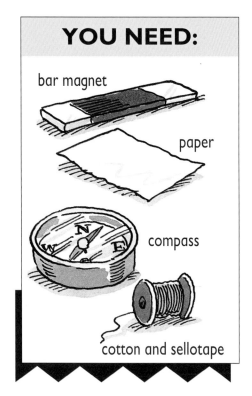

YOU NEED:

bar magnet

paper

compass

cotton and sellotape

✦ Make a paper sling like the one shown in the picture.

✦ Put the magnet into the paper sling.

✦ You will need a compass to look at, but do not put it near to the magnet.

✦ Watch the magnet. It will slowly spin until one end is pointing north.
That end is the north pole of the magnet.

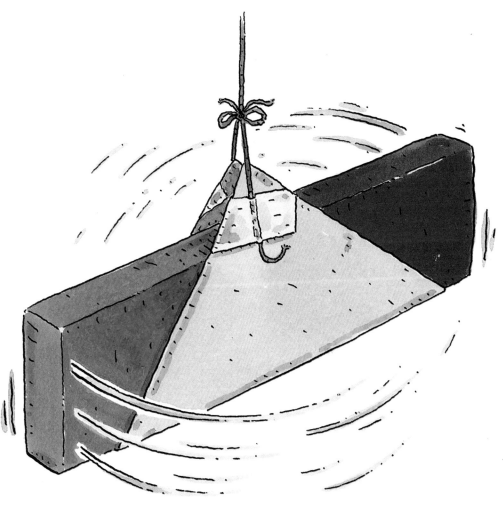

Do not put your compass near to the magnet

Now try this

Task 10 *Magnet against magnet*

✪ You know how to find north on a bar magnet.
Now take two bar magnets and find north on each.

✪ Put a small sticker on the north pole of each magnet.

✪ Use the magnet to find out what happens when:

      north pole is against north pole

      south pole is against north pole

      south pole is against south pole

      north pole is against south pole.

✪ Write down the rules about **magnets** attracting and **repelling** each other.

Finding the poles

⚡ Where do you think the poles are
on these magnets?

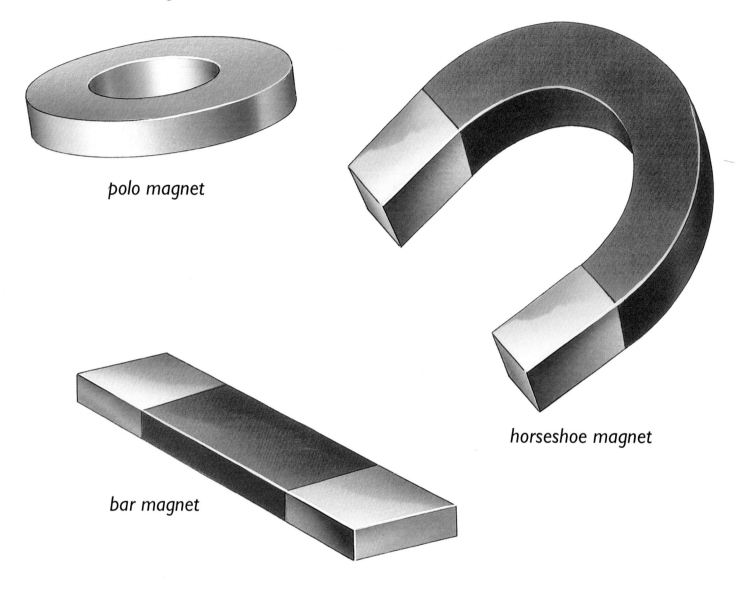

polo magnet

horseshoe magnet

bar magnet

button magnet

magnetic marble

⚡ How do you think that you could find out?
Write down your ideas.

⚡ Now try out your ideas.

Amazing magnets

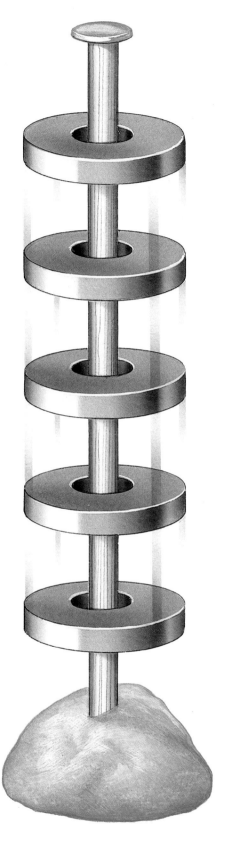

✿ Make some polo magnets bounce up and down on a stick.

▶ **Think about**

Why do the polo magnets bounce without touching each other? How could you make the polo magnets stick to each other?

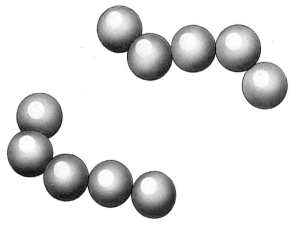

✿ How do you think magnetic marbles work? Explain why they stick.
Draw or write to show your ideas.

✿ Draw or write to show some different ways you could use magnetic marbles.

Magnetic forces in action

 Look at these photographs.

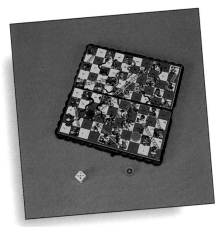

Think about

Why are magnets used in these places?

 Write down your answers.

Now try this

 Make your own magnet.
Photocopy Master 8 shows you how.

YOU NEED:

a team of Star Investigators

paper-clips

magnets
and other things to
make your model

Industry Challenge

✪ In the canteen at Star Ltd, they are losing a lot of knives, forks and spoons.
They are being thrown away, by accident, with the scraps of food.

✪ Can you design, make and test something to stop this happening?

✪ HINT: in your model use paper-clips instead of knives, forks and spoons.

✪ The directors at Star would like to know how you solve this problem.
How will you show them in an interesting way?
In your group, give a presentation to others about how you solved the problem.

YOU NEED:

cardboard and other materials

paper-clips

some real or pretend cheese

see-through jar, plastic lemonade bottle or fish bowl and water.

plastic toy figures

magnets

string

Magnetic Challenges

Try these challenges.

✺ Challenge 1

Make a magnetic maze game.
Get the mouse to the cheese.

✺ Challenge 2

Make a magnetic diver in a bottle.
How will you make the diver go up and down in the water?

✺ Challenge 3

Make a magic paper-clip trick.
How can you make the paper-clip stay in mid-air without touching it?

Challenge 4

Make a magnetic puppet theatre.

Think about

How will I make the theatre?

How will I make the puppets move?

What story will I tell?

Show your play to the rest of the class or to younger children.

Design and make another toy which uses a magnet.

Draw your design on Photocopy Master 10.

Fact File

Special magnets

Did you know that ...
If wire is wrapped around an iron rod and electricity is passed through the wire, the rod becomes a magnet?

This special kind of magnet is called an **electro-magnet**. When the electricity is switched off, the rod stops being a magnet.

Electro-magnets are used in scrap-metal yards and on some special railways.
Why do you think these special magnets are used there?

YOU NEED:

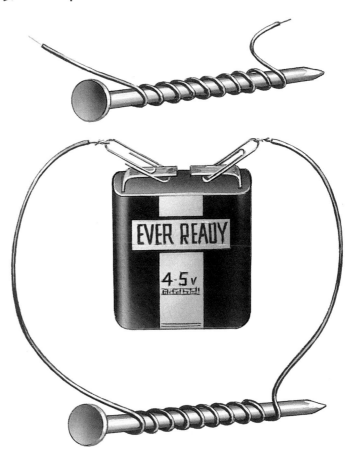

large iron nail

4.5v battery

paper-clips

wire

Task 16

Make your own electro-magnet

✦ Wrap the wire around the nail.

▶ **Think about**

What could I do to make the electro-magnet stronger?

 PCM 11

✦ Draw your ideas.
Write what you would do under your drawings.

✦ Now try out your ideas.
Which one was best? How do you know?

 Do not leave the electro-magnet on. It will 'run down' the battery.

Gravity is a force which pulls things towards each other.

 Task 17 *What is gravity?*

The children in the photograph are talking about the word **gravity**.

✸ What do you know about gravity?

✸ Try the activity on the next page.

YOU NEED:

some big strips of paper

⭐ Work with some friends in a group.

⭐ Each take a big strip of paper.

⭐ On the paper, write down what you think gravity is.

I think gravity is..................

⭐ Don't tell each other what you are going to write on the paper.
Keep it a secret until everyone is finished.

⭐ When everyone in your group has finished, show each other your ideas.

⭐ Were all your ideas the same?

⭐ Talk about your different ideas.
Who do you think had the best idea?
Why?

Fact File

Isaac Newton

Here is a story about gravity.

No one really knows if it is true, but it is an interesting story. Hundreds of years ago, a scientist called Sir Isaac Newton was sitting under an apple tree. The story says that an apple fell from the tree and hit him on the head. This made him think about an idea he had had. Newton thought that it was a force called gravity which pulled things towards the centre of the Earth.

Just think, if there wasn't any gravity, the apple would not have fallen off the tree. Even more strangely, it might have floated up towards the sky.

Gravity pictures

The pull force of gravity means that ...

If you drop a plate, gravity will pull it down towards the centre of the Earth.

If you throw or hit a ball into the air, gravity will pull it towards the centre of the Earth.

If you parachute from a plane, gravity will pull you down towards the centre of the Earth.

If you ski downhill, gravity will pull you down towards the centre of the Earth.

PCM
12

 Now draw four of your own gravity pictures.

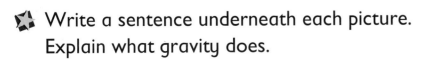 Write a sentence underneath each picture. Explain what gravity does.

Did you know. . ?

The Earth's gravity

The Earth is bigger than the Moon.
The Earth's gravity keeps the Moon
going around the Earth.

What do you think would happen if
the Moon was bigger than the Earth?

Fact File

The pull of gravity

Wherever you live on Earth, gravity is a force that pulls you down towards the centre of the Earth. It stops you falling off the Earth and flying into space. The Earth is bigger than you, so it pulls you towards it.

You can measure the pull of gravity on you by putting bathroom scales between you and the Earth. Gravity pulls you towards the Earth. The scales measure how much you are being pulled by gravity. Gravity is the same as weight.

The bigger the mass of something, the bigger the force of gravity and the more it weighs. The smaller the mass of something, the smaller the force of gravity and the less it weighs. Imagine that you could magically get rid of gravity. You would weigh nothing.

Now try this

Task 19 *Using gravity*

 Design, make and test a marble run like the one in the picture. The run should be no longer than 1 metre in length.

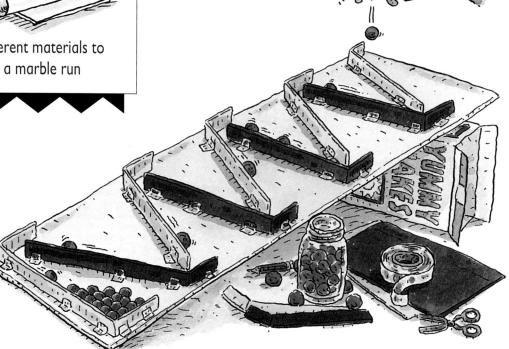

The run should be as slow as possible without the marble stopping.

YOU NEED:

some marbles

some different materials to make a marble run

Think about

How many different ways can you make your marble slow down?

Now try this

Task 20 *Force challenges*

Try the challenges on Photocopy Masters 13 and 14.

YOU NEED:

a team of Star Investigators

some materials to make a rocket and launcher

You will also need some elastic bands.

Investigation
Defying gravity

Design, make and test a space rocket launcher.
Use a planning board to help you.

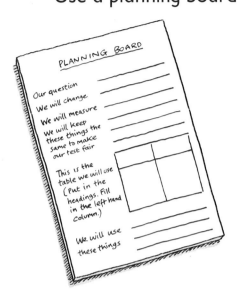

PLANNING BOARD

Our question

We will change

We will measure

We will keep these things the same to make our test fair

This is the table we will use (Put in the headings. Fill in the left hand column.)

We will use these things

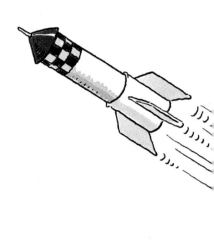

▶ **Think about**

Where is the force which will push it away from Earth?

Which force will bring it down to Earth?

What can we use?

How will we measure how far the rocket travels?

Gravity rap

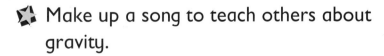

✦ Make up a song to teach others about gravity.

PCM 15

✦ Write the words on Photocopy Master 15.

✦ Put the words to music.

✦ Perform your song to the rest of the class.

Spot the
forces

Game

How many forces can you spot on this page?

List the forces you can see on Photocopy Master 16.

Summary

Revision (Key Stage 1)

A force is a push or pull. A push or pull force can make something start to move. A push or pull force can change the shape of some things.

Magnets can push or pull some things.

The bigger the push or pull force, the further something moves or the more the shape of something is changed.

A pull force can stretch things.

A force can make things slow down, go faster, or stop.

Key Stage 2 (Lower Junior)

Magnets can push or pull things without touching them.
Magnets can **repel** other magnets.

Gravity is a force which pulls things towards each other.